PURPOSE MATTERS

How the Power of Purpose Defines Our Life

James M. Morrison

www.OptioInstitute.com

Printed in the United States of America

Design by Andrew J. Siddoway
Chief Editor: Andrew J. Siddoway

Purpose Matters: How the Power of Purpose Defines Our Life
James M. Morrison - 1st ed.

ISBN: 978-0-9839434-2-6

10 9 8 7 6 5 4 3 2 1
First Edition

This book is dedicated to those searching for their purpose and true path of contribution in this life.

May we all examine our life to unlock our full potential.

——Table Of Contents

— Preface

In our day, it is not unusual to hear sorrowful stories of a young single mother working several jobs to keep her head above water. We often empathize with the misunderstood disappointment of children arriving home during the economic downturn learning that their father has lost his job and in a moments notice the children are asked to give up the activities they love. Our hearts ache from the sacrifices and hardships that bombard many people. Is it any wonder why most people are facing unprecedented battles to grasp life's gems and to admire life for its own sake?

The very demanding nature of life causes us to yearn for peace and relief. With insurmountable pressures and a buckling force of stress, the release from our hectic world in which we live is only found in discovering our individual purpose. The call to action of identifying our purpose is building within each of us, summoning our personal contribution.

Our approach to life's obstructions, our critical responses and behaviors, are predetermined by cementing our purpose deep into our souls. The following pages will take you through the seven days that allowed me to define what really mattered in my life and to establish my purpose.

Simply stated, ***Purpose Matters***.

Chapter 1

— I WASN'T READY

I somehow felt unprepared to meet Him in that defining moment. From a young innocent age, I knew my purpose in life and the path that needed to be pursued. I really knew no other roads that would lead to the full purpose and design of my existence but the one set before me through the instruction of my parents and all those who had an effect in paving the path of joy and peace in my life.

In calling for such a need as the power of purpose, the voice of one's life echoes the motivation to fulfill the authentic meaning behind their life. Individuals have accomplished wonderful achievements because of a clearly defined purpose, which awakened the willpower to see the opportunities of possibilities, to realize their full creation. Such knowledge of life unleashes the energy and the passion to drive one and pull others for a higher level of contribution in their mortal existence, and by extension, the eternal perspective.

The inevitable design of my life was to meet Him in His full glory with confidence that I had lived life as He planned. I knew in my accounting to the Creator, the law of justice and mercy would apply. These virtues appear to be in direct competition with one another rather in essence, they compliment each other. Mercy can't exist without applied justice; if there is no justice there will never be a need for mercy. The effects of these two virtues will never supersede His great love and caring outstretched hands, which provide support and unconditional love in the full measure of one's life.

At one crossroad in my life, I had great security of knowing in the ensuing heartbeats all of life's curtains would be taken up and my eyes would see Him. I had a wonderful feeling knowing 40 years of life culminated to this moment to meet the Savior. He is utterly incomparable as to who He is and certainly everything He has accomplished. All of my life experiences and accomplishments paled in comparison to my present moment of greeting Him.

In the course of my sense of meeting Him, I became deeply afraid of my interaction. The fleeting moment of security quickly transformed to despair and deepening shame. I originally assumed I had done enough and my character would shine brightly before Him. Regardless of how small or large, I internally realized my full design and purpose had not been lived.

Like so many of us, we all desire to leave a footprint on the pages of history. Helen Keller shares her perspective on leaving a footprint:

"I long to accomplish a great and noble task, but it is my chief duty to accomplish humble tasks as though they were great and noble. The world is moved along, not only by the mighty shoves of its heroes, but also by the aggregate of the tiny pushes of each honest worker."

It is not good enough just to live life rather we must live life with a distinct purpose and contribution. In the nature of life, it is simply not enough to complete one dimension such as a professional interest but rather what we feel and how we see the purpose of who we are; there exists other dimensions that create the whole person.

Lord Nelson lived the very principle of every man fulfilling his duty.

"On the morning of the bloody battle of Trafalgar, Lord Nelson stood on the deck of his battleship overseeing the massive destruction. Suddenly, a ball was fired and landed 15 yards from where he was standing and broke his spine. He laid helpless for three and a quarter hours until he died. Upon his impending death he said, "Thank God. I have done my duty!""[1]

We are divine beings with diverse talents and unlimited potential to add to the brilliant fabric of society. The texture comes in various forms based on the gifts we each received at birth. There is a noble comfort in fulfilling one's life before the day of accountability. The paths we choose tend to afflict each of us as we walk over and around the debris and obstacles placed before us. Most often we feel out of step as we try to follow our purpose in life.

In the despairing pain of all my deficiencies, I tried to hide my face. I remember pleading the is-

---

1. "Thank God…. David Howarth, Trafalgar: The Nelson Touch (New York: Atheneum, 1969), p. 150.

sue to stop the impending interaction of meeting Him. I panicked and started to run in the open space, which was filled with brilliant light. Such an effort to hide was hopeless because there was no place to cover me; everything was illuminated. I longed to feel the warm blood and cold snow that lay beneath me; only a return to the agony would bring comfort.

No matter the condition I was in; release from the spiritual fear would be a temporal reprieve. I desperately wanted to feel the pain and desperation of the accident that I once felt. The physical suffering I had plead to be released from prior to asking for relief by returning to heaven.

Chapter 2

—— THE POWER OF

INSPIRATION

What appeared to be another vague day on Tuesday, February 29, 2000 (a leap year) turned out to be a day not to be forgotten. I received an ordinary phone call from my brother-in-law Jeff to invite Chase, my soon to be 12-year-old son, and myself to accompany him on a snowmobile trip with his 11-year-old son Brenden. The phone call brought lots of excitement and justified concern. I had only been snowmobiling once many years before with a tour guide so this trip would require careful preparation.

Based on my inexperience, I had an impression that this two-day trip would require all of us to stand on the shoulders of each other since we had only two days to put all the details in order.

In the mind of Chase, there was the sports allure to take the risk of trying something new, to test the speed of a snowmobile, to fly off jumps, and to experiment with the power of avalanches. This, after all, became an obsessive challenge to brave the elements in the heart of Utah's bitter winter.

I hung up the phone and immediately told Chase to prepare for an adventure of a lifetime. We would travel 2 ½ hours south of Salt Lake City and snowmobile in a remote area of the Wasatch Mountains. Serendipity plays a role in Chase's life. In a moments notice, he was not only going on a snowmobile trip without his two triplet sisters, but also missing two days of school.

Unfortunately, to the uninitiated thoughts of my mind, inherent enthusiasm for the trip turned to unmistakable panic. At first glance, the thoughts of danger and death appeared to be irrational, even absurd. I attempted to force such thoughts out of the dark corners of my mind and redirect my focus on the purpose of our going on the trip, the purpose of strengthening a father and son relationship with Chase.

I strained to console myself by processing the logical knowledge of my previous snowmobile experience and the expertise of those who were going with us. However, the unrelenting inspiration persisted to grasp my attention. I concluded that this was not a fair contest. Chase was excited to go and I wanted to stay home. The struggle between logic and inspiration, at best, was a mammoth concern pressing down on me.

Inspiration is not an abstract sense rather it is a practical strength that comes from God's influences. The tidal wave strength behind inspiration provides truth to assist individuals in moving in the right direction to fulfill their purpose. Every individual is unique with their given talents to accomplish a very distinctive contribution in life. The conscious effort to understand the power of inspiration will generate a beautiful life with durable beams of meaning and produce outcomes that will build enormous benefits. Accepting the principle of inspiration and the source in which it hangs creates a natural power to carry the heavy weight of life. Harnessing inspiration is a source of authentic power.

Inspiration will open eyes with which to see and ears with which to hear. Its influencing power will inspire life and produce attitudes to have the wisdom to build a foundation of true purpose. One's individual will should never supersede the will of the Creator. The cause of inspiration will never diminish one's purpose rather increase the effects of life. The inspiration we receive ties our purpose to the will of the Creator.

Unfortunately, in the arrogance of many people, they feel that their abilities replace that of inspiration relying on their own power to guide life's journey. The consequences of such misunderstanding lead to unmet expectations, and in many cases, a life unfulfilled. The knot of unhappy events and negative consequences tightens when one does not act upon inspiration.

I heard the excitement from Chase as he went to bed. He asked me,

"Dad, do you promise that we will go on this trip?"

My reply,

"Of course, and we will have a great time."

As I retired to bed, my thoughts created awful scenes of the suspecting horror of going on a trip that was perhaps my final chapter in life. My sweet wife Trish leaned over to me and said,

"I'd rather you not go."

I assured her that it was fine and there was no better opportunity than to spend two days with our son one-on-one.

Chapter 3

——Prayer Provides Security

Certainly, the internal conflict of the trip kept me from falling asleep, which in turn permitted my mind to draft storylines of horror and tragedy which only cemented the wall of fear. The dilemma of the night was to find answers to the sharp pointed question: How was I to balance the commitment to go on the trip amid the profound feelings of inspiration not to go? In hopes of finding answers, I turned to my customary source of comfort; I started to pray.

We all have situations by which we need to rely on prayer; there are no exceptions. There exist in life those moments with destructive power that are beyond our capacity to carry alone. The whole world is in need of such council outside of our own advice; I was bound to find answers to my heavy issues. I believe that prayer is a powerful lift, which is the supporting component for peace and comfort through life's journey.

If there was ever a time to find a lift from the dark hole of my problem, it was in this moment. I have heard of such sacred stories where prayer was the key to finding truth. It is the vehicle to discover safety and comfort in the dark abyss of a problem. I needed to find the direction to ease the burden of my troubles.

With the knowledge of prayer, I asked the reason behind the promptings and more importantly,

"What should I do?"

I needed to yield to my feelings that the trip should be cancelled. I plead for strong understanding as to why but to no avail. It was not going to be by chance or by effort that the outcome of the trip would be in my control. As I continued to seek answers, it was stirred up inside that in the event I was to go on the trip, I would pass away. After hours of what appeared to be earnest supplication,

I received my answer. If I go, I would not be returning home.

Through the dismal lonely night I used a unique blend of persuasion and justification to protect myself from harm. I felt in my arrogance I could manipulate the inspiration by controlling the warring elements among the winter conditions. I would simply master the decisions on the slopes and put myself in places of confidences without compromising the intent of having fun snowmobiling. I pretended long enough in my pride that the plan rested essentially in the appropriate equipment. After all, it was a matter of fashioning a plan and controlling the conditions.

The view of ourselves most certainly affects our attitudes and behavior towards life. An arrogant and prideful approach makes us a ruler unto ourselves rather than being subject to such principles of inspiration and guidance, and furthermore, pits us against other people. If this is the case, we lose the ability to learn and lose the quality of all relationships. This position of life is ultimately self-defeating.

Life can be enriched significantly when precipitated by humility to understand that we are buffeted by conditions and that circumstances apply that are invariably beyond our control. An oft-related story is most people do not walk the path of life with an attitude of confidences because they don't have the inspired strength.

All the while, I was arguing the narrowly defined situations; my impulse had succumbed to being stranded on the mountainside in the frigid winter night and freezing to death along the side of my powerless snowmobile.

In feeble attempts, the comfort of safety would emerge out of the solution of keeping my brother-in-law in sight and in the incident of being separated; the outcome of a safe return depended on whether our two-way radios would work. If there was an opening to receive light and peace to my concern, it was in the solution of man made devices.

Chapter 4

—— The Desperate Phone Call

On Wednesday, March 1st, as the sun breached the horizon, I placed a call to Jeff. The single purpose of the call was to ask about two-way radios. Such a request can appear to be hesitation, if not insecurity, in the adventure. Because snowmobiling is not an extreme conditions sport, it was almost ludicrous to harbor such concern; however, to the inexperienced it caused for some uneasiness.

He answered the phone,

"Jeff, thank you for inviting us on the trip and is there anything I need to do? Oh! By the way, do you have two way radios?"

He said that he did. I quickly asked,

"What is the range?"

He responded,

"Seven miles."

With my imperfect opinion, certainly we should be safe. I was building perceived security based on the tools and decision making capabilities rather than accepting the fact of inspiration as power and to act accordingly.

I have since learned the following simple practice that would move people in a direction with greater strength for long-term peace. Our ability to do more and be whole in all the various dimensions of our lives will be more complete through the inspiration we receive. The orientation of inspiration flows directly into the pools of purpose as to what kind of person we should be and what we must do.

I spent the rest of the day looking in closets for snow clothes, goggles, and gloves. The identical outcome was repeated, while searching I could not find the items and when I did only one piece of the set was found. The day was uneventful but consistently frustrating. Given the day was dedicated to preparation I had little time to think about my persistent impressions. The important thing was to have everything packed and ready to go.

The awful evening of uncertainty in the trip resurfaced occasionally and levels of anxiety varied throughout the day. In one moment, there was comfort knowing I had made all the necessary arrangements; the next moment, it felt quite the opposite and the fluttering shallow breathes of panic prevailed. Although I endeavored to control the emotional fluctuations, the cycles created a whirlwind of uneasiness for my wife, Trish.

I never stopped dwelling on the tiring concerns of my mind and heart. Later that evening after the triplets Ashlee, Lohren, and Chase had gone to bed, amid my inability to limit my emotions, I sat on the bed and shared my feelings with Trish. Given the solemn mood of the circumstances, she started to softly cry. I realized too much emotion of high or low on either side could be counterproductive.

The problem with talking about my feelings is it would bring an amplified emotion of the reality of my being severely hurt or possibly killed. I reflected for a moment on what to say. What does anyone say when the message would deliver hammer like blows to the one you are addressing? I had explored every possible angle and started to express my feelings.

There wasn't much I could do, I bowed my head and held her tender little hand to bear her burden and to strengthen each other. What lay before us was the culmination of 15 years of love and understanding. Avoiding such a discussion could have perhaps disguised the emotions but would have unveiled a lack of trust.

The one thing that must be common in every relationship is trust. When considering all things, nothing is more important than trust. If trust is built, it has the potential to serve as a concrete foundation on which everything stands. Trust is the knot that ties people together.

With a chilled heart, idle breathing, and an inaudible voice, I simply stated,

"Trish, I feel my life is coming to an end."

Her vision blurred with tears and she quietly questioned,

"What are you talking about?"

Beneath the question was no valid exposed answer. I simply whispered,

"It was an illogical feeling and it meant nothing."

At first glance, such a conversation would naturally dampen our spirits but rather quickly turned to an affectionate moment of holding and calming each other. I extended encouraging words,

"It's going to be beautiful up there. Think of the moments I will have to talk with Chase."

In the midst of a kindhearted moment, the collective atmosphere continued to evolve into caution. I held her as she found solace in her sleep.

Chapter 5

—A Sad Good-Bye

After relentless prodding to align every thought throughout the night, I concluded that I could beat the odds of such promptings. Besides, everybody has insight into certain events. In fact, I had many prior inspirations where I disregarded them as my own thoughts. By now, this was something of my being insecure with the elements of risk and the conditions to brave the cold, wind, snow, and ice. To any other outdoor enthusiast, this would be an opportunity for the special blend of adrenaline and camaraderie with great people and magnificent panoramic views.

The root of inspiration lies deep in the power of discernment. It is the stem to direct our attention to those things with significant importance and to reveal exactness. Our conscious brain processes masses of information at any given point in our surroundings and the inspiration speaks to our sensitive souls; the emotions to act upon those things we feel to avoid the pitfalls or safeguard our direction in life. Once we learn how to discern, the choices we make will become easier.

I had confidence in my plan but I lacked the self-assurance in having complete control on the mountain. There are simply too many elements that are beyond my control such as the weather, terrain and degrees of slope all of which mean disaster. The smallest change of condition could trigger a serene landscape to transform into a bustling pool of snow forcing me to swim to the top. Avalanches were one of many concerns.

Irrespective of how hard I attempted to control my concerns, the cumbersome worries never ceased. Against the uncertainty, there was no serious consideration of not going. I had the desire to build a relationship with Chase. This precarious experience demonstrated my aspiration to develop a long-lasting influence with him, which was the powerful motivation to go.

I was naïve about heavens influences to assist me along the way. In the natural course of life, there are various obstacles and challenges. We all know a great deal about them. In the event of some unforeseen danger, and the unthinkable happened of not returning home, I needed to prepare Trish and the rest of the family for life without me.

The final source of security before we left was for me to put all the finances in one place. After Trish had left for school, the first task was to collect all of the appropriate documents from our investments to our liabilities. I found our insurance policies, the small amount that we did own in stocks and bonds, and the mortgage and credit card statements.

I began to mentally undo and redo the best place to put the documents and how to present them in such a destructive instance of her needing them. The most important thing was for Trish to find them without much effort. She undoubtedly would have other titanic issues to resolve with grief-stricken children. It quickly became clear the papers needed to be placed in the fourth drawer down in the dresser.

Some of life's greatest expressions of love and appreciation are found in a short handwritten note. Such a practice can create a dynamic interaction in a relationship that captures the very essence of how one feels. I will never forget the day when I wrote a few simple words with profound love.

"Trish, here are the finances. I love you."

This was my simple declaration of how I truly loved and adored her. I took the little note and placed it on top of the other documents and whispered,

"Good-bye Trish, I love you."

Chapter 6

—— THE PICTURE OF WINTER

In the set hazardous tone of the occasion, Chase and I gathered our bags to leave for the obscure insignificant portion of the world. The fingertip sensitivity of just leaving my last good-bye to my wonderful wife brandished self-defeat. The feelings I felt verged from one end of the spectrum of deep sadness to the other end of shrill mystic in the adventure.

The intense departure for our ill-fated trip had its effect. I reflected on the consequences of even the smallest misstep of merely not paying attention to details could be disastrous. Like so many of us, we have our own aspirations which we need to pursue but I didn't want to sacrifice my life on the alter of a snowmobile trip. Off we went to Fairfield, Utah a short 2 1/2-hour trip south with two fathers and two sons. We were all going to share one singular purpose, to bond with each other.

We entered into Sanpete County and rather than focus my attention on my concerns I chose to focus on those little things that are truly the big things. In reality, it's not so much about the large moments as it is the small enjoyment in the things that matter most in one's life. Time of enjoyment with Chase was the heartfelt cause of the adventure.

An awe-inspiring backdrop for the perfect painting depicted bright vibrant colors, which came forth from nature's canvas. The sharp yellow sun was warm; the white snow-capped pyramid tops were calm; the green frost tipped pine needles were docile; and every other brilliant and subdued color took their appropriate places in the illustration of winter.

Often, we can't embrace life for its own sake until we let go of the selfish thinking of making it about ourselves. When we make our lives about other people, the harmonious beauty all around is magnified.

The first item of business was to rent the snow-mobiles. Inevitably, upon walking in the rental shop we had high expectations to rent the largest and fastest snowmobiles available. We picked out our aggressive colored snowmobiles and all of the necessary equipment from the helmet, boots, and goggles to the non-essential facemasks and sun block for any unanticipated inhospitable situations.

We hitched up the trailer and headed to the motel. The motel was old and abundantly aged. Emblazoned on the exterior were the markings of severely damaged wood from harsh winter conditions and sun brittle planks of timber from relentless summers of the past. It was the perfect replica of a timeworn house from the old west settled in the mountains with notably extreme temperatures below freezing and intense heat.

We wrangled the door open and smelt ripened 100-year-old air. The musty carpet mixed with dungy beds provided a safe haven from the outside elements. The small room offered no moveable space for four people, let alone two double beds. There was a small, cold, and characterless bathroom, which required perfect navigation around the door and toilet to latch the door closed. In many different ways, we were determined not to spend any more time in the room than what was considered completely necessary.

The protective gear of tomorrow was nonchalantly thrown on the beds and we set out to find something to eat. As we walked across the street towards the only unadorned diner, the calm cold air coerced us to cover up with heads bowed and eyes on the austere moonlight peaking through the sheer clouds.

The environment of being in an unfamiliar place, and the cold blackness of the night skies caused me to become insecure. My thoughts were drawn back on my promptings I had the previous two days. I tried to escape their clutch, but I was bound by such strong impressions of losing my life. To say the least, I had no appetite for my traditional hamburger.

The feeling was deep, not only for me, but also for Chase. In route back to the motel, Chase asked,

"Dad, are you okay?"

My swift reply,

"Of course. Why are you asking?"

Undoubtedly, Chase sensed the heavy burden I was carrying. I reassured him that all was well.

Chapter 7

— THE WRONG ROAD TRAVELED

The paralyzing fear from the warnings of harm and the uncertainty of tomorrow continually strengthened my desire to be in the safe haven of my home. The culminating security one feels should come from the home. There is no substitute that provides the fertile environment for the growth of healthy productive people. While fighting the emotions, I reflected on the importance of planting seeds of well-being for everyone in my family. In my moments of despair, I yearned for the emotional refuge found within the walls of my home.

We prepared for bed but not without some concocted entertainment. Chase and Brenden represented the forgotten past of how fun it was as kids jumping from bed to bed. Youth is no inhibitor; they would see who could complete a 360-degree flip or the most creative gymnastic move. After the excitement waned, we did the usual nightly routine, retired to bed, and shut off the lights.

The calming effects of the light were now replaced by the unsettled darkness. Finding peace is parallel to the light from a superior source outside of our own capabilities. Every individual has the ability to draw upon the powers of heaven to find relief from their heavy burdens. I am convinced that the spirit is a part of the physical body and light comes from spiritual things. The quest may be extensive, but with adequate faith the light eventually fills one's soul. Cradled in the cocoon of my bed, I knelt down in prayer with the covers drawn to shield me from unwanted spectators. I was searching for hope and truth from a loving God.

Our sincere expression to the source of light allows us to unite with the perspective of God and to receive inspiration and direction to live life with greater purpose. With unfamiliarity to the light of knowledge most people relentlessly pursue their own shaded path, which causes many to stumble and fall. Such an approach and attitude is in direct competition with the central influence from the omniscient of all light and knowledge.

This experience created more awareness of the essence of influence, which in its greatest power flows from heaven. Unfortunately, in my undernourished understanding, I insistently positioned my way of thinking to go on the trip. Arguably, I presumed carving time out of my block of obligations to build a deeper relationship with Chase was the best approach. Regrettably, I exposed the both of us to great vulnerability and danger.

The actual interplay and conflict of my attitude created static in my communication with Heavenly Father. Such interference keeps the communication scrambled and indiscernible. I made this more about my will as opposed to His will. The arrogance in life is always out of place. How does one possibly expect to counsel the Christ on such matters when it was He who had the most difficult situation to endure? Jesus Christ knows what it is like to have friends abandon Him; it was He who healed the sick and diseased and fed the poor and hungry. We cannot council Him but we can seek His council. There is no greater gift we could provide to ourselves than to give our complete will to Him.

There must be, in the same sense, humility to

recognize the uncertainty beyond our understanding and knowledge. The masked events in our lives come in all shapes and forms and are often unrecognizable as to what they are. What I thought was best was a flawed interpretation of what was really worse. My appeal to Him was a snowmobile trip rather than listening to the promptings which were protecting my real purpose.

Morning quickly came and the snow-bound boys were ready to traverse along the slopes and race the open valleys. There was no perceived danger zone found within any of us that morning. As the early morning hours unfolded, chaos ensued in our preparation to get ready. Encapsulated in my duffle bag I saw extra underclothing. I attempted to soothe my fears and quickly thought,

> *"If there was a time where I needed extra layers of clothing to provide protection, it would be in this moment."*

Chapter 8

—— TODAY IS THE DAY

Based on our appearance, any passerby would be convinced we were the most experienced snowmobilers. Even with the skills lacking, the style of our dress more than compensated for the novice expertise. We had our snow pants, jackets, gloves, goggles, and helmets in hand. All fear was now stripped away. I felt I had done everything right. I had prepared with the correct gear and I furthered my chances of safety by securing two-way radios in the remote event of being separated from the rest of the group. Furthermore, adding layers to my security beyond my clothing, Jeff had been snowmobiling on this same mountain two weeks earlier. We were set for a trip on the Master's canvas painted by the strokes of His hand.

Realistically, with preparation preceding success, what could possibly happen? There was nothing that was likely to occur because of the solid foundation I had built over the past two days. The brick and mortar strengthened the attitude of invincibility; nothing would be able to stop us. All four of us were ready to stand victorious upon the defenseless mountain.

We opened the loosely warped motel door leading directly to the parking lot. I was just beginning to cross the doorway when I saw the two snowmobiles hitched to the truck. As my eyes zeroed in on the forbidding snowmobiles, my previous feelings and warnings funneled into one cataclysmic emotion of doom. The instant panic stole the air out of my lungs and I was forced to remind myself of the process of breathing. The only response I had was,

"Today is the day. Today is the day and I am not ready."

Any pleasant emotion descended far below the feelings of despair, loneliness, and anxiety. Questions continued to flow through my mind.

"What am I to do? How can I stop this from happening?"

The seemingly bombproof plan had instantly imploded my shelter of security. I wanted to run and disappear.

The strain of the emotions was becoming too unbearable. The decisive move, both away from my better judgment and spiritual promptings, towards the unpredictable forces beyond my control were far more attuned to catastrophe. Our stabilized footing would eventually give way to the slippery slopes as we got in the truck and headed up the ominous mountain.

The colliding inspirational attempts to get my attention had failed. I was plagued with terror from the thoughts of,

"We are not to be here! We need to abandon any intention of going to the mountaintop."

The critical decision to stop the trip seemed to have passed me by. We had intruded on the point of no return.

With trepidation suppressing my heart, we proceeded to unload the trailer. As the engines warmed up, we made the final adjustments: defogging goggles, tightening boots, and zipping coats. Trying to compensate pessimism with optimism, I took the driver position and Chase sat behind me. I looked at Jeff and he gave the affirmative nod and we took off.

In broad terms, what I needed to accomplish for the day was to balance fun with caution. Unfortunately, the required concern of safety led to unadventurous speed and mundane maneuvers. Despite my chameleon personality from exciting to dull, the weather was picture perfect: bright golden sun, calm crisp air, brilliant blue skies, and fresh fallen snow.

Chase wanted me to give an ambitious thrust by opening the throttle. Finally with great encouragement, I tilted my wrist and we flew across the snow. The powdered snow blew and the cold air turned our faces into red frosted ice. We were enthused by the prospect of hairpin turns and cliff hanging ridges.

I learned that when optimism and confidence run high it could be destructive. Nonetheless, I never allowed our spirits to run too high with the hopes of decreasing the chances of recklessness. The larger-than-life sport of snowmobiling was the potent weapon in controlling the terrain and harrowing conditions. Our excessive willingness of waltzing with risk on the dance floor of fun peaked when the snowmobile oddly shutdown. This was now a symbolic prompting. It was time to take note.

Chapter 9

— LACK OF COURAGE

With the passing of sequential events, the broken snowmobile fit perfectly in its chronological order. Perhaps this was the greatest disappointment for Chase. Without appearing excited for the situation, I said,

"We have to do something. We will get it to work!"

The attitude of we will "Go For It" was all but

gone. It was now the opportunity to act consistently to the feelings I was having over the past three days. It was time to go home. I had beaten all the promptings and warnings. With great exuberance I quietly shouted without saying a word,

"I did it!"

Jeff and Brenden came to our rescue. Jeff was always the optimist telling us not to worry. With my sparse support, Jeff quickly diagnosed the problem. The undercarriage protecting the engine was damaged. Without an engine guard, snow would pull up into the engine and kill the motor.

The final bolstering for Chase's faltering spirit was Jeff's prompt recommendation,

"How about getting another rental? You can have a new rental in one hour."

As Chase built new hope on Jeff's comment, I quickly disassembled my comfort of returning home. The encouragement of getting another snowmobile naturally withered my already shrinking spirit.

The more I listened to the plan of replacing the snowmobile, the more I realized the trip would not be cut short. Before limping down the mountain with a crippled snowmobile, I mentioned how much fun we already had and getting another snowmobile was too much of a problem. In a feeble attempt to change the plans, I recommended we pack up and go home. In short, we could stop for lunch on the way and be home before dark. They must have not detected the necessity in my voice of wanting to be home.

Jeff quickly responded,

"Oh no, we need to get another snowmobile because after lunch we are heading to the backcountry."

This was the significant moment to stop him from going down the hill and getting another machine but the threshold quickly past. Indeed, in some strange sort of way, by not saying anything more I subconsciously supported the replacement. We sputtered our way to the trailer. The contradiction of my physical hands helping Jeff load the wrecked machine was in direct competition of what my mental appetite was trying to accomplish. At this juncture, I endorsed the trip into the backcountry.

I learned the outward strength of one's character is the courage to do the right thing even when it is not popular. Character develops from one's purpose, which provides a sense of being and a direction to awaken the willpower to do the right thing. A meaningful life stands concretely on a foundation of beliefs and firm core values. When circumstances seem to be ominous and extenuating challenges insurmountable, it is the purpose of an individual that provides the strength to bear the adversity.

I remained with the two boys to eat our sack lunches while Jeff went to town to exchange snowmobiles. The lull of the afternoon break slightly dissipated as the boys threw snowballs to pass the time. In what appeared to be minutes, one hour had come and gone. Upon Jeff's return, the quiet rest quickly turned to busy activity to recoup the time we had lost on our backcountry expedition.

Chapter 10

— THE UNTHINKABLE
HAPPENED

There were countless opportunities to turn the hourglass of fate, but the present time was to get on the dreaded snowmobiles and go. If I were to return to this very place later in the evening, it would be a gift.

Like all gifts we receive, they must be received with appreciation. Through my hallmark inspirations and promptings, my willingness to listen and to act upon such impressions was put to the test. The outcomes would surface from the fortified faith to believe. I promised Chase that he could drive the snowmobile after lunch. He assumed the driver position but I felt I needed to drive until we arrived in the backcountry. Before I knew what was happening, Jeff and Brenden had disappeared into the white canvas leaving behind a compass of freshly laid snow tracks.

Not surprisingly, I started to panic. My worst nightmare was about to unfold in a series of unpredicted events. Those seemingly important two-way radios were now going to save my life. Focus transitioned into disarray as I thought:

"How could I possibly find them? How would I get back?"

My concentration was centered squarely on starting the machine. I vividly remembered the black electric start button on the right throttle underneath my large gloved thumb. I desperately tried to start the snowmobile but each time it failed. It was a hammer like blow to my spirit when the snowmobile failed to start.

"What does this mean? Was it another sign to stop the inevitable?"

Everything that had transpired the last several days was a quiet war with myself. Nothing was easy. If there were to be another opening of disappointment, I would just call it a day. In a stupor, I looked at the throttle and realized a switch labeled OFF and ON. I was thankful for discovering my problem and in my embarrassment I flipped it to the on direction.

In the potential clash of His will and my will, the wrong decision was made. I pressed the starter button and the muffled sound and oily smell of a healthy snowmobile pierced our senses. Time retracted to an unusual pace and rested on the back of a snail. My undivided attention centered exactly on the design of the handlebars.

"Who would possibly manufacture a steering system with a ¾ inch bar connecting the left handle to the right handle?"

Common sense would typically lend itself to knowing such a design could hurt the snowmobiler.

With an inability to subdue my concern; I refocused my attention on Jeff's newly formed tracks; the need was to gain time on those ahead of us. I no longer muddled around with the speed of the snowmobile; I opened the throttle to feed the engine with an abundant flow of fuel. We flew across the sun reflecting snow bouncing and tossing for seven miles.

Even then, in the midst of all my worries, the fusion of speed and slight loss of control was better than slow and total control. The goal was to find Jeff and Brenden much sooner than slightly later. My concentration was precise and my heart rate plateaued from the firm resilience to find them. The alternative of not finding them was not even a consideration.

With a sigh of relief, we saw Jeff and Brenden 40 yards off to our left coming towards our direction. What a sight to see their snow covered faces and arms in celebration of our catching up. What appeared to be a heartfelt celebratory return was nothing more than a frantic warning of extreme danger. This was not a cruel disillusionment but a desperate attempt to change our course. I quickly looked down at the speedometer marking 70 MPH. My worst nightmare unrolled into a scroll of reality and the unthinkable happened.

Chapter 11

— A STIFLED CRY
FOR HELP

My solo performance had not only staged a tragic ending for myself, but Chase's life as well. I learned that my life has significant purpose and meaning and I am the creative force behind it. Each of us has a unique purpose to accomplish significant things and to become more than what we are currently. Without this perspective, life becomes hollow. Healthy and happy lives are those led by individuals who spend their time and energy fixed on the activities that have eternal consequence.

Activities that are not meaningful and have little significant value need to be subordinated to the strength of one's purpose.

The moments of warning had past and our once grounded machine was sailing through the open air. The snowmobile flew unrestricted at 70 MPH with the opposing ice bank serving as the runway, 40 feet below. In my weak attempt to pull the front end up from its downward spiral, I stood with one leg pushing on the back with arms coaxing the front. The bullet strength force plunged the snowmobile directly into the path at the bottom of the icy wall.

The impact of the steering column, with its imposing ¾ inch bar, hit squarely into my stomach, severing my organs. With such bludgeoned force, time quickly stood still; the stimulus of my surrounding became heightened. With what I thought was my last release of oxygen, I let out a long drawn moan. My ice-cold expression of agony was interrupted by warm blood running down my face.

A sharp piece of the windshield was embedded in my chin and indescribable pain in my internal organs prevailed. I was disemboweled with my small intestine severed in three places and large intestine in two places. Additionally, I burst open my stomach and bladder and ruptured my appendix. The once powdery snow was firmly compacted as I laid helplessly underneath the snowmobile

Immediately, the agonizing physical pain gave way to the excruciating emotional pain for Chase's safety. Helplessly pinned under the snowmobile, I attempted to call out his name, which was like yelling in a sound proof room. As I vied to be heard, I yelled his name once more and yet again quiet whispers echoed from my screams.

My heart plunged as I felt Chase was severely hurt, or worse...dead.... There was no chance of reversing time. The inevitable was going to happen. I felt a draining of energy and my body was falling asleep. I offered a simple prayer pleading with the Lord to allow me to return to my heavenly home. When the last portion of energy was diminished, the throbbing pain of my injuries found rest and I was in a state of peace.

A feeling of comfort came upon me and I knew that we are never forgotten in life or in the hereafter and we matter to Him. Life continues and the temporal knowledge remains an important part of who we are. I had full recollection of every aspect of my life, which seemed to be compressed into one continuum. I remember saying:

"I am liberated...I am free."

My life was a complete whole without divisible parts, with perfect clarity, and in precise detail. Without effort, my mind accelerated in the ability to think. I had perfect recall of every human interaction and an overwhelming ability to process information faster than a computer.

Concerned with the temporal well being of my family, I reviewed all of the financial figures I had left in my drawer for Trish to find. I was simultaneously adding seven sets of eight digit figures such as $146,214.13 and subtracting accumulated debt of $13,437.67 all while calculating the correct figure. This was done all in the same thought.

Suddenly, I was being beckoned by the voice of Chase crying and asking me not to leave. The momentary relief from pain was overcome as my core pulsed with profound intensity. It was unbearable and I needed relief. Chase urged me to hang on and he would get help. In the dark corners of my mind, I quietly asked,

"What have I done?"

The countless influences during the previous days were to keep me from this tragic experience; oh the folly of pride. Relying on my depleting levels of strength, I mumbled,

"Chase, I must go. You are the man of the house and I want you to take good care of mom and the girls. I love you."

Fatigued from emotions I slowly closed my eyes.

Chapter 12

—— IT WAS MY TIME

The natural tendency was to excuse myself from the distressed surroundings. The pain decreased as it did before. Although I felt liberated from the physical world, I could not see anything other than an all-encompassing radiance of perfect white light. It felt as though I was surrounded by the warming presence of light.

The force moving me forward allowed me to feel as though I was about to meet the Creator of heaven and earth. There was something indescribably special in the posturing of meeting the One who has served as the ultimate purpose in my life. The inclination was to run and reach out towards Him. My mind felt more powerful and unconsciously, but realistically, I had full recollection of whom I was and furthermore, what I have done in all the horizontal areas of my life from being a young boy to being a husband and father.

Reaching back through the pages of my personal history, I was reminded of my inappropriateness in all facets of my life. My mind reverted to those moments where I had been unkind, dishonest, angry, or prideful. The feeling of peace and light that surrounded me quickly turned to pandemonium and darkness. I knew I had not fulfilled the total measure of my purpose nor was I prepared to meet Him.

I had to desperately stop the impeding interaction. Perhaps I could hide and not be seen but I had no place to go. I would rather turn back to the horrible condition on the mountainside and deal with the accident than to meet the Savior unprepared. I cried out,

"Please, I pray that I can experience the pain and warm blood".

My petitioning was filled with a quivering voice of urgency.

Between the ends of emotions from joy to desperation, I awoke with Jeff holding my face with his frozen hands, reassuring me he would do everything possible to hike me out seven miles. I was so thankful for two frozen hands on my shivering face. Reflecting back to the possibility of losing my life, an internal desire ignited to live life in a deliberate fashion, more importantly, to correct all my wrongs.

Unbeknownst to any of us on the trip, there were two men in the area that were avid snowmobilers who felt impressed to remain on the other side of the gully to possibly assist someone in need. I am thankful those two men were humble enough to understand the influences from heaven. On the top of a distant mountain there were inspired men who acted on such promptings even when they made no logical sense. If individuals follow this principle of inspiration it will openly appeal to their true purpose.

Jeff instructed the two boys to head down the mountain in waist deep snow and brisk wind to find the road. With the aid of the other two men, Jeff lifted me out in a fireman's carry on the back of his snowmobile. During the rush to help, the once snow capped mountains and green painted pines disappeared into the background of discomfort.

The scores of events over the last three days had me lying in the backseat of Jeff's SUV. He raced down the hill in hopes of finding a medical center in a small remote town and against the uncertainty; we picked the boys up along the way down the hill.

The prospect of getting to the hospital and the more decisive action was to do it with great urgency. In my weakening state, I asked Jeff to pull over for I was dying and I wanted to go peacefully. The energy had all but left me and I felt like I was falling sleep. I knew it was time for me to die. Jeff was adamant and insisted I hang on since we would be at the hospital in a few minutes. I quietly replied,

"No Jeff, It's over".

Then the most miraculous thing happened—the kind that moves me to understand the healing power of one another. With one hand on the steering wheel traveling 90 miles an hour down the canyon, Jeff reached back to hold my hand.

Chapter 13

— THE FIGHT FOR LIFE

The kind of strength that was manifested through the power of Jeff's touch was evident. There was a true healing power flowing into my being. I learned that physical touch is a power that can heal not only physically but also spiritually. It is the most attuned sense that we possess as human beings. It is the largest organ and touch, when applied appropriately, heals broken bodies and souls. We all need to feel the goodness of each other and the love that emanates from one person to the other.

Clutching Jeff's hand controlled my fears and provided a resurgence of energy to do as he asked, hold on to life. He drove faster down the hill knowing the endeavor was truly a matter of life or death. He pulled his hand away for minutes at a time to regain control of the canyon road; every time he removed his hand, the feeling of falling asleep returned. Far beyond my will to survive, I wasn't able to cope solely on willpower. I moaned for Jeff to pull over; the groans reminded him to once again grab my hand. Even though he had no idea where to find a medical facility, he would say,

"Hang on, we are almost there."

We arrived at a small local clinic but the resources at the facility were adequate for the typical casual illness and injury but not for such trauma. A helicopter was called immediately to transport me to the closest hospital in Provo, Utah, over 70 miles away.

I was strapped to a gurney board and loaded into the helicopter. The restrictive straps robbed me of my ability to move my head, arms, or legs. The only movement available was my fingers and feet.

I vividly remembered four people being on board: the pilot, copilot, and two nurses, one at my feet and the other by my head. I was in a state of being extremely faint and losing the strength to hold my eyelids open. The far more difficult task at this point was to stay awake because going to sleep equated to imminent death.

Although there was a great amount of encouragement given to me, the only task that separated me from the other side was merely closing my eyes and giving up. Regardless of how badly I wanted to welcome the warm peace of returning to my heavenly home, I needed to fight and finish the purpose of my life.

I was able to indistinctively hear the distraught communication of the nurse speaking with the hospital staff in Provo, Utah.

"We are losing the patient. There is virtually no blood pressure!"

There was not much left they could do. In my motionless body, I had to send a life-saving signal that I was faintly still along for the fight. I tried to wiggle my fingers and move my feet. The best effort I could give was to move my pinky along the side of the nurses pant leg.

Chapter 14

——Thirty-One Minutes Is Too Late

With the distressing conversation, it became obvious to those on board that I was not going to live through the short 30-minute trip to the hospital. I continued to fight the best possible fight of my life. In the end, it was the will to survive far more than the force to give in to the weakness of a failing body. I needed to supplement my surrendered body with inner strength and expand my spirit to hang on. There was no time to show any weakness and say good-bye; this struggle had eternal consequences. Surprisingly, my meager scratching of the pant leg must have been enough for them not to give up on what was a plausible failed rescue.

Upon arriving in the Provo hospital, the most conspicuous observation to my doctors as they opened me up was the 70 percent of blood supply bleeding out into the cavity. At first, according to their intellectual instincts they were about to raise the old proverbial white surrender flag; when they saw the extensive damage, this was much like walking through the valley of death.

They began to unpack the badly bruised and swollen organs and laid them on tables and strung the large and small intestines throughout the operating room. They spliced, attached, and sewed the stomach, bladder, small and large intestine, and removed the appendix. Too few people are given the chance to relive life with a new eternal perspective. As I woke up in the intensive care unit following surgery the next day I was given that very chance.

Combine the promptings and inspiration of the past three days, there was harm clearly around the corner and my pride obscured my view. Pride is one of those intangibles that put human beings against all other character traits: forgiveness, respect, consideration, love, understanding, empathy, and forbearance. In the book, *Mere Christianity* by C.S. Lewis, he writes,

"Pride gets no pleasure out of having something, only out of having more of it than the next man...It is the comparison that makes you proud: the pleasure of being above the rest. Once the element of competition has gone, pride has gone."[1]

The general measure of how one is loved is the dimension of how people come to the assistance to one another; family members from different parts of the country surrounded me. My identical twin brother Bruce was in Cancun, Mexico and had not yet arrived. Weeks later he expressed the actual reason for his late arrival. Based on the initial dire prognosis from the medical staff, of my not making it through the cold dreary night, he wanted to deal with my passing alone. Nothing more needed to be said. We knew we loved each other.

My mother was sitting by my side holding my hand, my sisters rubbing my feet, and Trish caressing my face. Oh how I love them all. Out of their empathy of understanding they realized the needs to rescue me from the harshness of the accident. My parents, brothers, and sisters: Michelle, Donnette, John, Bruce, and Maridon and all my sister and brother in-laws showed great nuances of love by their touch, words, and compassion. And

1. "Pride gets no: C. S. Lewis, Mere Christianity (New York: Macmillan, 1952), pp. 109-10.

not only had my family come to my rescue but also Trish's family and my young children Ashlee, Lohren, and Chase. They provided me strength and love which is the greatest healing source. Although it was an extraordinary day being surrounded by family; I slept through it.

The dramatic episodes of the following days ingrained the uncertainty of life in my very soul. Two days after my original surgery, the unthinkable happened. The traditional quiet Sunday afternoon came to an abrupt end; my blood pressure quickly dropped to dangerous levels.

I felt as though I was once again flirting with the end of my time. The internal source of energy started to leave my body and the physical functions started to fail. As I was losing consciousness and passing away, there was immediate pandemonium with doctors running down the hall, my gurney at their side, yelling to clear the path, and my father-in-law, Ron, giving me a blessing.

Chapter 15

—— THE POWER
OF PURPOSE

The changeable and volatile situation had
me flat on my back and returning to the operating room. The overarching environment implied
varying degrees between life and death, I was going to either be healed or die. The doctors were
gripped by the sense of urgency rushing down the
corridor. To capture the full scene, I have often
wondered what it would have been like to be the
spectator when there were frenetic responses with
everyone on the floor. And, here I was the star of

all the drama.

Virtually in all the layers of injuries, it was soon discovered my internal organs had grown three times the size and a mesenteric artery leading from my heart had burst open. They had to make more than a token effort to save my life. Those observing in the operating room started to unpack the organs and commenced sewing up additional perforated holes and closing the broken artery.

On the basis of what the surgeons learned, they summarized the injuries:

> *"His organs look like ground hamburger. I doubt he will make it. Have his family come."*

Due to the fragile state of my body, every minute that passed was checked off as victory over a battle. Life hung in the equilibrium of will and science.

While resting alone in my dark room on Sunday evening, I would find my conscious mind lost in the maze of my life's experiences. I could no longer camouflage the past events of my life rather I could only unveil the real purpose of my existence.

> *What is my unique endowment? What are my talents? Who am I to be?*

While the actual answers of the questions varied broadly from a responsibility to my footprint in the path of history, I needed more time to fulfill my divine purpose. I was desperate to live life with full purpose; my life had secured powerful meaning.

Unfortunately, under the crushing weight of such questions, I felt that my life was coming to an end; the stopwatch of life was going to cease operating. The physical pain was vast and my spirit distraught. In desperation to find help, I peered out the window where nurses typically observe their patients and saw a man walking past the large plate of glass.

With no reservation, I called out to him. There was something extraordinary about that man that conveyed he represented everything good. I asked,

"Please hold my hand."

I reached out to touch his hand; I was able to tap into his spiritual strength, which healed my broken spirit.

The power of touch was healing my physical body and my spiritual soul. I felt the power of strength flowing into my being as if I was attached to a power outlet; it was an increase in power. In the manner in which he expressed his love and concern through his touch, it allowed me to find peace and fall asleep.

I have reflected on those moments when the power of touch has the influence to heal people physically and spiritually. This was not a mere co-incidence because of the experience I had while laying in the back seat of the SUV coming out of the mountain.

While holding the man's hand, I was reminded of the scriptural story from the Bible in Matthew. The woman with a blood condition was on the ground among the multitude trying to touch the hem of the garment of Christ when virtue left Him. The power of touch healed the woman. This story goes hand-in-hand with my experience.

Often we find the need to share our life-changing experiences. With what I had learned, I took the opportunity to share my experience with others in the hospital. I asked for all those who had attended to my needs to come to my bedside. I told them of my experience the night before. I said,

"I am thankful for the wonderful technology and the knowledge to heal but never underestimate the power of touch."

As I shared my thoughts, they expressed the same truth of love providing the power to heal. Many of the doctors and nurses said,

"When all else fails, we hold our patient's hands and miracles happen."

I shall never forget all the experiences of those two weeks. It was an event that dramatically taught me transforming principles to live life deliberately and to become a person of true purpose and design. There is no greater gift we can give ourselves than to discover our divine purpose and contribution yet to be made.

We are destined from the Almighty on high to increase our full measure. The all-encompassing power of purpose matters as we embark on life's greatest journey; the journey of not only discovering our purpose, but the great triumph of living to our full potential.

After two weeks in the hospital it was time to come home. As I entered my house, my place of security and peace, I began to cry,

"I am home.....I am home."